B.R.

Why We Have
THANKSGIVING

Why We Have
THANKSGIVING

Margaret Hillert

Illustrated by Dan Siculan

MODERN CURRICULUM PRESS
Cleveland · Toronto

Library of Congress Cataloging in Publication Data

Hillert, Margaret.
  Why we have Thanksgiving.

  (MCP beginning-to-read books)
  SUMMARY: Relates the journey of the Pilgrims to America and describes their struggles during the first year that culminated in the celebration of the first Thanksgiving.
  [1. Thanksgiving Day—Fiction. 2. Pilgrims (New Plymouth Colony)—Fiction] I. Siculan, Dan. II. Title.
PZ7.H558Whi [E] 80–21431

ISBN 0-8136-5604-4 (Paperback)
ISBN 0-8136-5104-2 (Hardbound)

    8 9 10   96 95

I want you to go here.
You have to do what I want.
Go here. Go here.

We do not want to go there.
We do not like it.
We want to do what we like.

You can not do what you like.

Get in here.

Get in here.

This is the spot for you.

We do not like this.
Oh, we do not like this.
What can we do?
What can we do?

We can go away.
Yes, we can go away.
That is what we can do.
We can go in a boat.
A big, big boat.

Come on. Come on.
Get this on the boat.
We have to have it.
Work, work, work.

Oh, what a big boat!
We will go on it with
Mother and Father.
We will go away on it.

Here we are on the boat.
This is fun.
Away we go.

Away we go.
But where will we go?
What will we see?

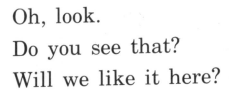

Oh, look.
Do you see that?
Will we like it here?

Look up, up.
Look at that.
Do you see what I see?
How funny.

Come on.

Run, run, run.

This is fun for us.

Fun for you and me.

I guess Father and Mother
did not like it.
Here we are on a boat.
Now where will we go?

What is this spot?
Is it a good one?
What will we do here?

We have to work.
We have to make a big
house for boys and girls
and mothers and fathers.

Oh, this is good.
Now Father can make
a house for us.
We can help.
See what we can do.

Look out. Look out.

Who is that?

What will he do?

Help! Help!

Why, he wants to help.
What a big help he is.
This is good.

See this come up,
and this,
and this.
It is good to eat.

And here is something
to eat, too.
Something little and red.
Something good.
We can get some for
Mother and Father.

Now, sit down. Sit down.
It is good to have
something to eat.
It is good to have friends.

Margaret Hillert, author of several books in the MCP Beginning-To-Read Series, is a writer, poet, and teacher.

Why We Have Thanksgiving uses the 73 words listed below.

a	father(s)	like	that
and	for	little	the
are	friends	look	there
at	fun		this
away	funny	make	to
		me	too
big	get	mother(s)	
boat	girls		up
boys	go	not	us
but	good	now	
	guess		want(s)
can		oh	we
come	have	on	what
	he	one	where
did	help	out	who
do	here		why
down	how	red	will
	house	run	with
eat			work
	I	see	
	in	sit	yes
	is	some	you
	it	something	
		spot	